COLDPLAY

First published in Great Britain in 2005
by Artnik
341b Queenstown Road
London SW8 4LH
UK

ISBN 1–903906–73–3

Design: Supriya Sahai
Pictures: Live Photography
Book Concept: Nicholas Artsrunik
Editor: John McVicar

Printed and bound in Spain by Gráficas Díaz

COLDPLAY

Alex Hannaford

artnik books

acknowledgements...
I first met Coldplay backstage at the V Festival in
2000 when I interviewed Chris Martin for the
Evening Standard. At the end of April I interviewed
them again - this time for the Big Issue. In that
short space of time their star has risen to such
giddy heights it looks like there is no stopping
them.
Meeting them in person made writing this book a
whole lot easier but I'm also grateful to the
following publications and websites. In no
particular order:

The Times
Sunday Times
The Independent
Independent on Sunday
The Sun
Birmingham Post
Los Angeles Times
The Guardian
Washington Post
Daily Telegraph
Chicago Tribune
Daily Mirror
Edinburgh Evening News
Daily Post (Liverpool)
Sunday People
South Wales Echo
The Express
Express on Sunday
Western Morning News
Evening Times (Glasgow)
The Scotsman
Coventry Evening Telegraph
Evening Standard
Daily Mail
EMI pictures
www.nme.com
www.rollingstone.com
www.rockonthenet.com
www.coldplay.com
http://www.coldplaying.com/
http://www.easytoplease.net/

http://www.hotandcoldplay.com/
http://www.pleasureunit.com/coldplay/
http://www.justspies.com/
Brian McGee and, espcecially, bedwetters everywhere

Thanks:
As always, the staff at the British
Library. And Court, for putting up with
all this madness.

For Pat and Pete

COLDPLAY
A RUSH OF BLOOD TO THE HEAD

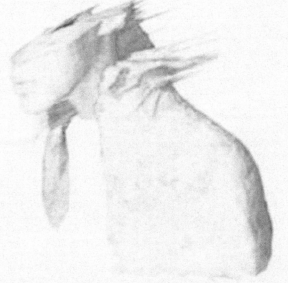

It's the year 2000 and a 23-year-old Chris Martin is sitting cross-legged on the patchy grass, fifty feet behind the towering second stage at the V2000 festival. Scratching his head and squinting at the sun, he sips on a small Evian bottle and smiles:

> Sometimes I think I'll quit next year *cos* I don't know how we're going to match this ascent. Has it happened too quickly? Have we cheated or blagged it? Are we really any good? We've got to prove ourselves more, know what I mean?

Our album's good, but it's not *Revolver*.

Chris is worried he isn't going to be able to top the songs on the band's debut album, *Parachutes*. He is worried he is going bald. In fact, he worries about almost anything.

Sitting in the August sunshine, Chris is surprisingly reticent about Coldplay's promising future, even though they'd just charmed several thousand people at the festival with their anthem '*Yellow*'; their debut album, *Parachutes*, is still riding in pole position in the charts and they've been nominated for the Mercury Music Prize.

There's just no pleasing some people.

But five years is a long time in rock 'n' roll.

Fast forward to 2005 and by the end of April, Coldplay have just become the first British band since The Beatles to have a new entry inside the U.S Top Ten singles chart. 'Speed of Sound', the first song off their new album *X&Y*, charted at number eight – the first time since the Beatles landed in the top ten in 1968 'Hey Jude'.

Chris Martin is relaxing in an armchair in London's Metropolitan hotel next to guitarist Jonny Buckland. The pair have just finished their third studio album, *X&Y*, and although in the last five years Coldplay have become one of the biggest bands in Britain, Chris is both cocksure and, yet, pessimistic.

He's an anomaly. Married to one of Hollywood's biggest stars, the father of a beautiful daughter, and one of Britain's most talented songwriters, yet he's still plagued by the fatalism of *it-could-end-tomorrow*. Nowadays he doesn't really think that, but he likes the act... it keeps his ego grounded.

At the moment we've got no ideas, so as far as I'm concerned there will not be another Coldplay record. But in two months time things might be different.

Even the title of their new album – X&Y – Chris says, reflects this 'tension of opposites'. He clarifies, 'As a band we survive by being confident but also by never thinking it's quite good enough.'

Another thing Chris has battled with over the past five years is a morbid fear of going bald. In 2000, to stimulate growth, he had his huge mop of curly locks cut off and he has continued to sport the kind of hairstyle that has come to be his public image. As he continues to think that a short haircut will promote hair growth, he obviously must still worry about going bald.

I thought I'd be bald by now and I'm very impressed that I'm not, but I still worry.

It is incredible that a band who have seen their star ascend to almost unreachable heights still have their feet on the floor. The editor of *NME* claims Coldplay is the best British band working at the moment. 'In terms of the records, their sheer hard graft, the column inches that Chris

Martin's love life [with Gwyneth Paltrow] is getting and the intensity of their live performances, no other band is even close,' he wrote.

Maybe they have the old adage 'pride comes before a fall' ingrained on their consciousness. By tempering their occasional arrogance with a realistic acknowledgement that it could all end tomorrow – whether through writer's block, media criticism or loss of fans – they seem nevertheless to keep churning out songs, their fans happy and the music critics off their backs.

Unlike most Hollywood celebrities who never seem to have had a 'normal' life before fame embraced them, Coldplay did and this hinterland of normality is still available to them. It is also one that fans can relate too, which makes their success all the more admirable.

Chris Martin was born on March 2nd, 1977, in Devon in the South West of England. His mother, Alison, was a teacher, and his father, Anthony was an accountant and part-time magistrate. Chris was the eldest of five children and the Martins lived in a large Georgian house in the picturesque village of Whitestone, a few miles from Exeter. From the hills dominating the village you could see all the way to Exmouth and Honiton.

Chris's grandfather, John Martin, had made a fair amount of money from the sale of his caravan sales business, Martins of Exeter, and the extended family were well-liked in the neighbourhood. They were hard-working, and Anthony and Alison instilled in their own children the values to which they themselves adhered:

...good manners, competitiveness and hard work.

It was a close-knit community in which the local pub, the Royal Oak, acted as a leisure centre. Chris enjoys his pint but has never been a heavy drinker. Anthony and Alison were involved in their local evangelical church, Belmont Chapel, and Anthony passed on his love of cricket to Chris and his two brothers Alex and Richard. Chris was an all-rounder and, since the age of sixteen, had turned out for his local side.

He was sent to Sherborne school in Dorset where he boarded and excelled academically. The school, which dates back to the early eighth century, says its aim is to be 'the school of choice for those who seek an all-round high quality education, based on Christian principles, in a non-urban environment,' and that it seeks to 'draw out the individual's talents and interests and to open doors for the future.'

Its better known alumni include the mercenary Tim Spicer, journalist Nigel Dempster, Oscar winner Jeremy Irons, Hugh Bonneville who was in Notting Hill and Iris, and the ITN correspondent Tom Bradby.

Although Chris enjoyed school he always preferred coming home to Whitestone where he would sit behind the family piano and play tunes he had written, or work out the notes to songs he had heard on the radio.

At the age of 15 Chris was listening to Neil Young, Tom Waits, Bob Dylan and U2. He would day-dream of becoming the next Bono, and began playing keyboard in various bands at school.

One of these was the Rockin' Honkeys – a rhythm and blues outfit. Chris played keys but desperately wanted to be the frontman. 'I used to try to steal as much attention as possible,' he said, 'even to the extent of wearing a leather waistcoat with nothing underneath.'

There are videos going around that really should be destroyed. They're hilarious - I'd really like to see them... then burn them.

Chris learnt a lot from that band. He was becoming proficient on the piano but his range was limited. He would spend hours at home listening to classics like Sitting on the Dock of the Bay and Pappa's Got a Brand New Bag so he could bring them to the band. He also tried to write songs of his own but he always felt they were too cheesy to show his band mates.

Jonny Buckland was born to teacher parents in London but at four years of age his family moved to the historic market town of Mold in Flintshire, North Wales. Like Chris, Jonny picked up an instrument at a young age and became proficient after hours of practice. His weapon of choice was the guitar and Jonny would try to mimic the riffs on his dad's Hendrix or Clapton albums. He was a quiet, unassuming lad, loved football, and had a growing passion for the indie music that was fast becoming an obsession for his older brother: **My Bloody Valentine**, **the Smiths** - he'd listen to everything. But then Jonny discovered **The Stone Roses** - a band that would inspire him to take his guitar playing seriously and maybe one day even form a band of his own.

Guy Berryman was born in Scotland, but was brought up in Kent, a typically English county, with its picturesque villages and legacy of historic castles. His mother was a teacher and his father, an engineer. Unlike Chris and Jonny, his love was for funk music and rare groove. Like the other pair he had picked up his instrument – the bass guitar – at an early age and practiced with all the dedication of someone who was determined to be a professional musician.

Will Champion, who was born in Southampton on the South coast of England, was a multi-instrumentalist. His great love was the guitar but he was also a good percussionist and in addition could play piano, even tin whistle. His parents, who were teachers, encouraged him to work at all of them. He went to Cantell School in Southampton and then Peter Symond's College, Winchester.

After A-Levels, Chris applied to study ancient history at University College, London. It was a big move, from the sticks to the city. Exeter has a population of 113,300 and is a far cry from the hustle and bustle of London.

Call it fate, but it was a move that would lead to the birth of what would become one of the most successful bands in the world.

Jonny, Will and Guy had applied to study at University College, London too, and they met one another in 1996 during fresher's week.

Will studied anthropology; Jonny, maths and astronomy, and Guy entered the school of engineering.

Chris and Jonny were in the same university halls of residence. After Chris discovered Jonny played guitar, that was it - almost immediately they were writing songs together. Chris had a back

catalogue of unrealised melodies and lyrics. He freely admits that before he met Jonny he was just half a musician. Both musically and personally the pair jelled. 'I think I'd been going through a big cheesy patch,' Chris said. 'Meeting Jonny removed a lot of cheese from my system and when we sat down and wrote together it was immediately better than anything I'd written for the eight years preceding.

Two and a half years passed before the pair would ask Will and Guy to form a band. The songs had to be right before they could play them to anyone else. The foursome would head off to lectures during the day and rehearse three to five hours a night.

They decided to call their band Starfish, and the first rehearsal was in Jonny's bedroom in January, 1998. Guy decided to drop out of engineering school to concentrate on the music but the rest of the band were determined to finish the degrees they had started especially as they only had under a year until their finals.

Although extremely versatile, Will was primarily a guitar player but, as the band already had Jonny on guitar and desperately needed a drummer, he was persuaded to play percussion. He bought a full drum kit and taught himself. Chris would later say 'As a musician, Will's got the most amazing sense of melody. He can play just about anything.'

The band rehearsed as much as their university schedules would allow.

When they broke through, Chris reflected to one journalist on the contingency of success: 'The one thing that keeps me grounded is that I realise my whole life is resting on things that happened to me, things I had no control over... meeting teachers who encouraged me, having a piano in the house, the fact that Jonny lived three floors down from me at university and, and then meeting Will and so forth.'

This kind of self-deprecatory comment is a defining feature of his personality.

Their first gig was at Camden's Laurel Tree on the 14th March 1998, not far from the World's End pub, but within a few months they had progressed to the nearby Dublin Castle and the 12-bar club.

Chris's childhood friend Phil Harvey offered to manage the fledgling outfit. He had promoted some club shows while studying at Oxford, but that was really the extent of his music business experience. When he got the job as Starfish's manager, Phil began reading a biography of U2 to give him some idea what to do. But first the band would have to change its name. Starfish just didn't sound right. Their friend Tim's old band was called Coldplay which he took from a book of poetry.

Their friend Tim's old band was called **Coldplay** which he took from a book of poetry. They would steal that name – after all, he wasn't using it any more.

They would steal that name - after all, he wasn't using it any more.

'This is what's so extraordinary about it,' Chris said. 'It's just like these five blokes, four of us and then Phil, who just know what we like and we don't know anything else. . . We're just kind of guessing our way through it.'

Coldplay's first major show was at Dingwalls on the banks of London's Camden Lock. Phil took on the mantle of chief organiser. They relied heavily on the support of their friends from college at that time and thankfully they managed to pack out the venue.

The band had six songs under their belts when they read about In The City - an 'unsigned' music festival in Manchester. Since 1992 In The City had attracted names like Malcolm McLaren, Brian Eno and John Kennedy. During the day, the music industry conventions were forums to discuss the business side of things. In the evenings it was time for new bands to shine, and possibly pick up that elusive recording contract.

Phil stumped up the cash so Coldplay could make their first recording – the three-track *Safety* EP, recorded at Sync Studios in Tottenham, north London. Previous bands that had trod its boards included Bernard Butler, Shane McGowan and Afro Celt Sound System.

The tracks on the Safety were 'Bigger stronger', 'No More Keeping My Feet On the Ground' and 'Such a Rush'. Just 500 copies were pressed, which Chris laconically admits they were hard-pushed to shift...

We struggled to sell those 500 copies – our mates were very tolerant...

But Phil sent a copy of the *Safety* and a brief CV of the band to the organisers of a small but prestigious venue call In The City.

They hired them.

It was a nerve-wracking experience all-round when they took to the stage at Manchester's tiny Cuban Café in late September, 1998. However, the stress lifted the music and the audience wouldn't let them leave the stage.

Among the audience was A&R scout Debs Wild. She was so impressed by the four-piece ensemble that she recommended signing them to the head of A&R at Universal Records. 'It's quite well publicised that I was the first A&R person who wanted to sign Coldplay,' Wild later recounted.

Unfortunately, the powers that be at Universal didn't agree with her. Nonetheless, when Coldplay went mega and Universal got egg in its face, Debs salvaged something more than a *I told you so* from the debacle. She explains, 'The decision went out of my hands but I did introduce them to their eventual publishers and lawyer.'

The lawyer was Gavin Maude and he specialised in music contracts and a recording contract was all Coldplay needed for their undoubted talent to blossom. Meanwhile, the band members studied at university, while continuing to play gigs in their spare time at the various sweaty venues around Camden.

At one of their many shows was Simon Williams, ex-NME hack and co-founder of the indie label Fierce Panda. The Panda, as it was known, was famous for finding the most promising acts in the country, putting out first singles by Supergrass, Ash, Placebo and Idlewild. Williams snapped up Coldplay in an instant and through his label the band released their first EP proper, *Brothers and Sisters*, in 1999.

By that summer, things seemed to be happening at lightning speed. The Brothers and Sisters EP was played on Radio One by DJ Steve Lamacq and the band suddenly found themselves with a small but loyal (and gradually expanding) fan-base. And it hadn't escaped the attention of the bigger record labels.

Later that year, just a few months before they sat their finals at University College, Coldplay signed to the major label Parlophone - a subsidiary of EMI. The label's bigwigs were more than happy to acquiesce in Coldplay's demand to sit their finals before devoting their lives to Coldplay... they knew that this was a band that was in for the long term.

'I'm glad we waited, actually,' Will commented. 'You can never tell how long things are going to last in this business, so it's good that you've got something to fall back on if it all goes pear-shaped, which has happened to a lot of bands.'

Chris too was philosophical. 'We got signed before we left university. It was great. But the thing that made us was the fact that all our uni mates came to our gigs so there was this tremendous buzz beforehand.'

At the time of the breakthrough he told one journalist in wonderment:

I'm just some public school boy with my house colours... I've got a degree, I'm from a middle-class family in Devon, I've got no story. We're just a bunch of students. I don't drink, I don't take drugs, I don't smoke. I can't be compared with Liam Gallagher or The Sex Pistols.

Martin will probably never appreciate that everything ends anyway and perhaps, as another man sang, he should learn to '...enjoy it while you can'.

A hard liquor-drinking, chain-smoking rock 'n' roll star Chris Martin wasn't. Well-educated, intelligent, spiritual and sincere he was. But at least he drank the odd pint.

Coldplay's first release on Parlophone was another EP, entitled *Blue Room*. It included two tracks from *Safety* - 'Such a Rush' and 'Bigger Stronger' - as well as three new songs: 'Don't panic', 'High speed' and 'See you soon'. By this point, the media was catching on, and although the rather unhelpful comparisons to **Radiohead** and **Travis** had already been aired, critics were almost universally positive. At least at first.

The Times said Coldplay impressed with their debut EP.

Its five tracks demonstrated a sense of poise and grace from a band who clearly appreciate the value of subtlety over raw power.

The *NME* said it may have been the ideal debut and claimed 'it saunters into your consciousness' and 'quickly snags in your memory. Very Nick Drake. Very English.'

Just before Chris, Jonny, Will and Guy headed into the studio with engineer/producer Ken Nelson to record their first album for Parlophone, tragedy struck. Will's mum, Sara, a lecturer at Southampton University, died from cancer. Before Will was born, she and her husband Tim had, in 1972, moved to Southampton and had been affectionately known as the 'pop star of archaeology' on the university campus. She had seen Coldplay perform live but died before their debut album was recorded.

The recording sessions were painful. Not only had Will just had to deal with a family tragedy, but all four friends were fiercely independent and together they were perfectionists. They made a pact that unless everyone was in agreement that a song should definitely make it on the album, it would be dropped.

Six agonising months were spent labouring over every guitar part, every vocal line. 'There must have been six times where we just sat around and everyone was just staring at the floor,' Chris said. 'It was not gonna get finished. . . But we kept chipping away. I thought, "Well, if we put this much passion into it, someone's got to like it." Something this painful can't be a waste of time.'

Parlophone released Coldplay's first single, 'Shiver', in March 2000, and Britain started to prick up its ears. Could their debut album possibly be as good?

'Shiver' reached number 35 in the UK singles charts. The band hadn't agreed on a track listing for the album yet but 'Shiver' was a perfect introduction to Coldplay, and it quickly became a radio staple across the UK. With their debut album almost ready, it seemed everything was resting on the follow-up single to Shiver. And if 'Shiver' was responsible for getting Coldplay recognition from the 'indie' crowd, *Yellow* would penetrate the living rooms of the rest of the country...

...middle England was suddenly listening to Coldplay as well.

After the release of 'Yellow' – a song that had 'appeared' to Chris after someone at the recording studio told him to come outside and 'look at the stars', the press were unanimous; Coldplay were a breath of fresh air. The *Birmingham Post* said their '...bitter-sweet brand of indie rock has been a ray of rare sunshine on the music scene during a cruel, cruel summer. They might lack something of the rock 'n' roll *je ne sais quoi*, but they're personable enough and have made very good on their early promise of being able to carry a decent tune.'

'Yellow' was the perfect slice of melancholy guitar pop. From the opening acoustic strumming to the first lines 'look at the stars/ see how they shine for you', you knew it was going to be massive. And it provided the ideal soundtrack to those winey, al fresco summer evenings.

Bands from the UK find it increasingly difficult to 'break' America, but 'Yellow' entered the U.S mainstream when the ABC television network selected it as its official promotional song.

Parachutes made its debut in July 2000, entering the UK charts in the coveted number one spot just a few weeks after its release. No one could have predicted the speed of Coldplay's rise to fame, and *Parachutes* spent the rest of the year hovering in the top ten.

The Sun, the UK's biggest-selling daily paper, climbed on board. Dominic Mohan wrote in July, 2000: 'Looks like Coldplay's superb album *Parachutes* is destined for the No. 1 spot. Midweek chart figures show it's way ahead of Eminem's *The Marshall Mathers LP*.'

Shortly after Parlophone released *Parachutes*, the album was nominated for the highly regarded Mercury Music Prize. It was up against albums from artists such as Nitin Sawhney, Kathryn Williams and Death in Vegas, but was ultimately pipped to the post by Badly Drawn Boys' *The Hour Of Bewilderbeast*.

Chris: We would be gutted if we hadn't been nominated, but we're also embarrassed because we were. It's a lot to live up to.

'I didn't know how seriously to take it,' Will said. 'I found it very weird that there were 12 or however many records, completely different in every way. I don't understand how anyone can even start comparing them and saying which ones are better than the others.'

Either way it was an achievement to have been nominated. And the industry and fans were in agreement: *Parachutes* was one of the best records of the year.

The Guardian commented that back in March the band was 'little more than a glint in their publicist's eye', but six months on 'Coldplay are front page news, with a top five single (the exquisite 'Yellow'), a number one album (the equally enjoyable *Parachutes*), a Mercury Prize nomination, and a major headlining UK tour to their name.'

It was nothing short of remarkable. Although it may have been two years since Tony Blair fanfared it for 'Cool Britannia' – proclaiming Britain was the coolest place on earth – here was the first British band for ages that was going to show the world what Blair meant. At the time, however, very few people realised just how big Coldplay was going to become.

Meanwhile the band was still battling with the **Travis/ Radiohead** comparisons, and took every opportunity to set the record straight. 'I don't really care to be honest,' Will told one interviewer.

The simple fact is that our songs are different and that's what should matter.

He continued, 'There's not really a category for the music that bands like us, Travis and Radiohead play. If you're a country singer you're a country singer, but there's no label for our type of music, unless its Jeff-Fran-Thom-Healey-Yorke or something. It's just the way that people make sense of things that don't already have an existing label I think.'

That summer, Coldplay was invited to perform at the V music festival. Sitting on the grass that August afternoon in the summer of 2000, Chris was in a contemplative mood. 'We just weren't prepared to accept failure,' he told me. 'We still won't. I went through college to meet my band mates. And I'm so grateful for that. We won't last forever, I know that. But we're about to do our own gig at the Shepherd's Bush Empire and that to us is like – wow. That's the sort of thing that makes it all worth it. Who cares if we're not around in a year's time. We're around now, so we may as well enjoy it. But at the same time it's really weird for us. At the moment I can't imagine doing another album but that's the nature of it I guess.'

If Chris hadn't listened to his father, Anthony's advice, he would have given up on Coldplay long before. 'We had thought about splitting,' he admitted, 'but it was never to do with band differences – well, once or twice – but right now I don't know what the future holds. If our next single doesn't do well, is it downhill from there? It's a really confusing time. Are we just doing well because there aren't that many other bands around. I do think we're really good because I listened to some of our album today and I actually really liked it.

'I'm a worrier, basically,' he admitted. 'I'm always wondering how we can improve; how we can validate our new-found status?'

Mid-way through the interview Chris spotted a girl who had held a Coldplay banner aloft during the band's performance. 'Look, there's the banner lady,' he said 'We've got to go and say hello to her.'

Oh man, that banner made it for me – I felt like I was in a proper band.

Back then there was still a sense of bewilderment and wonder at what was unfolding before him. This was truly an incredible thing that was happening to him and for that, Chris seemed genuinely grateful.

However, it doesn't take much to trip a bout self-deprecation and angst. This is the real Chris:

If we lived in the Big Brother house, I'd definitely be the first to be evicted because I smell very bad,

He laughed, then went back to his hair thing. 'Plus I'm always talking about going bald – I piss everyone off because I'm constantly worried about losing my hair. I wouldn't care about it if I wasn't the frontman.' Sometimes people tell him that if it all drops out he can have a hair transplant, but he is not sure about that either. 'Too Elton Johnish.'

Fear of baldness is one of Chris' favourite neuroses for parading before journalists to impress them with his vulnerability and ordinariness.

Only a year or so before my first interview, Chris was sporting big, curly locks on his head. 'One day I thought, why not cut it off. I wish I still had it though. But I guess with all these genetic things they're doing now we'll soon be able to have whatever hair we want. I've just got to sell enough records, so I can afford it.'

Again, Chris pulls out his cultivated split personality: he is alternatively self-congratulatory and pessimistic, sometimes to an alarming degree. 'Our album [Yellow] is really good and it's one of the best albums this year,' he noted. 'But Bob Dylan at his peak was producing two albums a year of infinitely superior quality in songs and lyrics. His output was enormous – it was just brilliant, and so natural.'

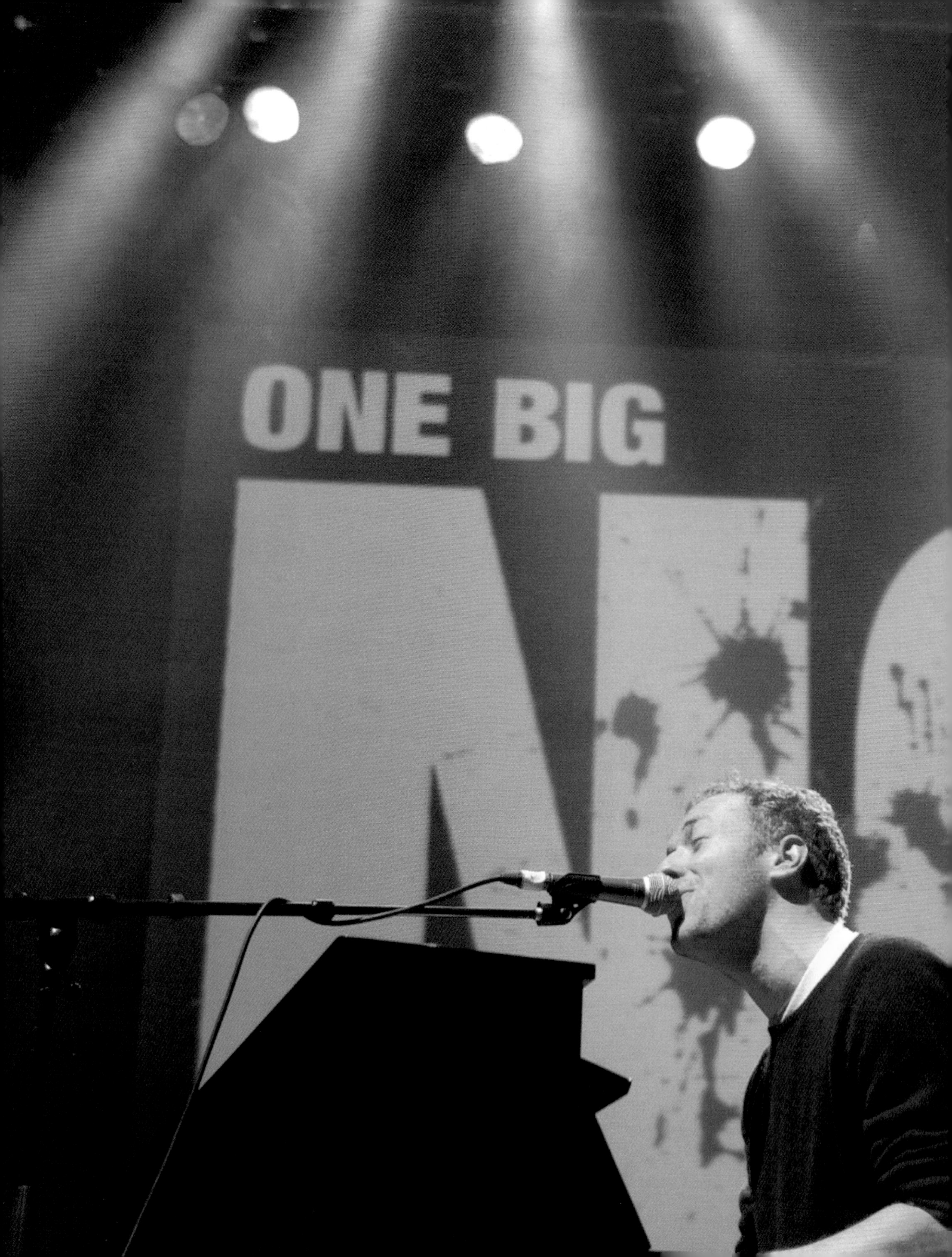
ONE BIG

One minute he'd put down his lyrics: 'I often think to myself what is *Yellow* actually about?', and the next he'd defend them: 'I know what it's about – it's about devotion. I've always felt that colour is hopeful and optimistic.

'But it's when you get people saying 'well, what the f*** does that mean?' that makes you question everything. But what's a 'Wonderwall', do you know what I mean? I just think it sounds great. And people are crying out for good songs.

'I think there have been a lack of passionate songs. It's rare you find someone like Liam Gallagher – he is incredible. A lot of the Oasis lyrics don't make much sense but he's singing with so much emotion. I love that. Wayne Coyne from the Flaming Lips, too. He sings with such conviction.'

I don't want to come across as sounding earnest or 'old muso', but it just strikes me that it's criminally wrong every time a young kid turns on the radio and hears Britney Spears for the umteenth time.

He laments the fact that there is a huge catalogue of classic songs that just does not get airtime, but he rushes to show his appreciation for the airtime Coldplay gets.

'I think radio is great for making a band because it's immediate. We've had loads of radio play and I'm eternally grateful for that. So many great bands haven't had that.'

And so, for the fledgling Coldplay, the songs were the most important thing. They had already, in such a short space of time, become known for their incredible – and indelible – melodies. Their songs were things of beauty and formed the soundtrack to our lives in the late 1990s: the breakups, the romantic evenings in, the road trips, the holidays and the weekends away.

Live, the band were determined to keep their concerts intimate and wait awhile before headlining a festival. 'I'd like it to seem we've still got somewhere to go,' Chris said. 'Headlining a festival is the pinnacle of your career and we want to always feel like we're improving and have something to aim for. At the moment we're still finding our feet.'

Will then interjected,

Hopefully we're never going to do stupidly big gigs.

He, acknowledged that festivals were a different kettle of fish. Their ideal venue, he said, was the Shepherd's Bush Empire – not so big that it loses its intimacy. 'I don't want to go any bigger – certainly not yet, and hopefully not ever.' That was one wish that wasn't going to be granted.

But even though *Parachutes* had gone platinum just four weeks after its release, not everyone was patting the band on the back. From some corners they were criticised as being 'careerist'. Alan McGee, the man who discovered Oasis and founder of Creation Records suggested their audience was made up of 'bed-wetting' school kids.

'It's not something that bothers us – it's a bit sad,' Will said. 'When you consider Oasis, who kept back songs from their first album to put on their third, and are now on their fifth, and Primal Scream, who've been going for 18 years, I don't understand how that's not careerist. But it's not something that we've deemed worth talking about.'

Will didn't seem to be aware that he had just been talking about it.

'We're starting to feel that everyone's out to get us,' Chris told the *Independent on Sunday*'s Nicholas Barber. 'The more people that like us, the more people seem to hate us... And it's something nobody tells you how to deal with. Then, as he prone to do, Chris pulls out his social conscience.

We're not evil politicians, trying to swindle the whole world.

Chris, as if you didn't know, doesn't rate politicians.

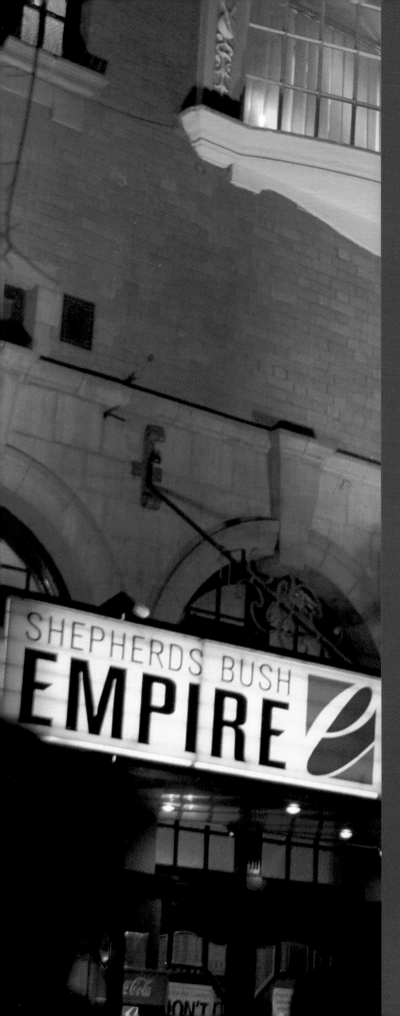

Despite the occasional snide put-downs, Coldplay were determined not to let that get them down. Their touchstone was the music – that was the most important thing. And as long as there were people out there who liked what they were doing, they would keep writing and performing. Chris, Jonny, Guy and Will didn't want to dwell too long on what McGee meant by his 'bedwetters' jibe. They knew their songs were heartfelt, at times even sentimental, but for them the melodies were what it was all about. And they knew they were incredible. Although constantly fleeting between optimism and anxiety, in a moment of uncharacteristic immodesty, Chris asserted:

I can tell you exactly why people like us: it's because we've got good songs, and we mean it.

He told Lyn Barber, 'The other day I met Liam Gallagher and he just doesn't give a shit about anything except songs. He loves music. And I thought, that's wicked, that means I don't have to feel any shame about it.'

Coldplay's gig at the Shepherds Bush Empire towards the end of the year 2000 only served to cement their place in the British consciousness.

The Sun claimed they were one of the UK's 'must-see' live acts. Dominic Mohan said of Chris: 'The packed front rows of frenzied females at the gig on Monday show he is fast becoming a major sex symbol.' It wasn't far from the truth – but a sex symbol was something that Chris himself would have found laughable.

But Mohan hit the nail right on the head with his signing-off comment:

Coldplay are going to be around for a very long time.

At the gig Chris joked with the audience about the Travis comparisons and managed to turn a faulty keyboard into a talking point between songs, endearing himself and his band to the audience even more. But they were already sold on Coldplay.

By the end of 2000 the band had received the *Q Magazine* Award for Best Album and had signed to U.S label Nettwerk for North America. The lads were exhausted. Endless promotion, interviews, appearances and touring had taken its toll. This wasn't what Chris, Guy, Jonny and Will were used to this, but it was something they were going to have to get used to... and quickly.

'There's a Bob Dylan film called *Don't Look Back*,' Chris remembers, 'and in it he's really having a go at this guy from the press, but the press is big part of it. I hate talking about myself all the time because it makes it feel a bit soulless, but I know it's got to be done. And I know I really love reading about Bob Dylan or Oasis or whoever, so I have to acknowledge it's about the whole package – it's not just about what you look like or what you play on stage.'

Success for Coldplay came comparatively quickly in the UK. Next stop was the USA.

The boys were confident they could crack America and they weren't at all bothered that a lot of British bands before them had tried and fell by the wayside. The days when a band could piggyback on the legacy of Beatles and Stones had long gone by the time Coldplay began strutting their stuff.

They were willing to put in the legwork, tour the 50 States, live out of suitcases, give interview after interview, sign countless autographs and speak to hundreds of radio DJs about life back in old Blighty, but so had been most of the other also-rans who'd stumbled and been humbled by the challenge of America.

Courtney Taylor, lead singer of the Dandy Warhols, had told Chris at the V2000 festival that Coldplay should tour America – 'They're really crying out for good songs over there.'

Chris reflected:

We just want to make one more record and try to make it the best record ever made, and then retire. I'll become a busker then, I think.

But before Chris could retire, he had Coldplay's debut U.S tour to attend to – scheduled for February 2001.

The *Washington Post* heralded the coming of Coldplay with adjectives that would have made Oscar Wilde preen. Their lyrical themes work from a simplified palette, the paper said,

...painting images of an impossibly fragile but corporeal world smudged with real beauty.

The newspaper said of their anthem 'Yellow' that it...

...traced the giddy delirium of newfound love, bringing to mind the ecstatic epics of early-'90s 'shoegazer' British bands.

America found the poetry to embrace Coldplay just as Britain had the previous year. Meanwhile, back on their home turf, Coldplay was shortlisted for a Brit Award and, even though the band was 3,000 miles away, they were still the talk of the town.

Coldplay's Los Angeles debut was at the Mayan Theatre on South Hill Street – a club famous for its authentic live salsa music. It is located in a beautiful, old pre-Columbian-style cinema where – so it's said – Marilyn Monroe once worked the joint as a stripper, circa 1948.

Coldplay was now a long way from the Laurel Tree or Dublin Castle in Camden.

For the tour, Coldplay's 'set' consisted of a small, illuminated globe, standing on one of their amps. It was a typical understated prop, underlining their leitmotif that the music was the most important thing. One reporter noted: 'At a time when so much of U.S commercial rock is taken up with paint-by-number anger and aggression, a band with its own voice and a down-to-earth approach is doubly rewarding.'

Another thing that was refreshing was the band's refusal to indulge in any rock star posturing. Chris commented enigmatically,

I spend more time not being a rock star than being a rock star.

The relentless interviews and gigging, while crucial for assuring Coldplay's imminent rise to superstardom, began to play havoc with Chris's health and the band had to cancel a number of shows while he nursed a sore throat.

By March, *Parachutes* had sold nearly 300,000 copies in the U.S, showing America had definitely turned on to British music again. But while the band's star was rising, Chris was feeling increasingly run down, even burnt out.

Every day their eleven-city U.S tour included back-to-back interviews and the obligatory radio station appearances. 'We're trying to break something that hasn't been broken in a long time,' the band's American label-head, Terry McBride, said. He added for the record, 'And it's not easy.'

Chris was cutting some interviews short and cancelling others altogether to rest his voice. He was also suffering from the rock singer's occupational hazard – tinnitus caused by persistent closeness to the banks of monster speakers. The main symptom is a constant and painful ringing in the airs, which in Chris's case made him double-up in agony. The long-term effects are deafness.

One particularly lengthy overnight journey in the tour bus was delayed by inclement weather and by the time Coldplay had arrived in New York City, Chris barely had a voice left. He then came down with 'flu.

He managed to film an appearance on the essential Conan O'Brien chat show, but that same night the announcement was made that the New York show had been cancelled. Rumours that the band were splitting dominated the latter half of their U.S tour as Chris battled flu and voice problems. They cancelled more American dates but the worst was still to come. Chris, Guy, Jonny and Will were due to head back across the pond for a European tour but Chris needed time to recuperate. The entire tour would need to be scratched.

It was a setback, but by summer 2001, all was well. Chris had recovered from his illness and the entire band were rested.They were booked to headline V2001 – ironic considering Chris had announced just the year before that headlining a festival would seem like the pinnacle of Coldplay's career.

As it happened though, this wasn't even close to the pinnacle.

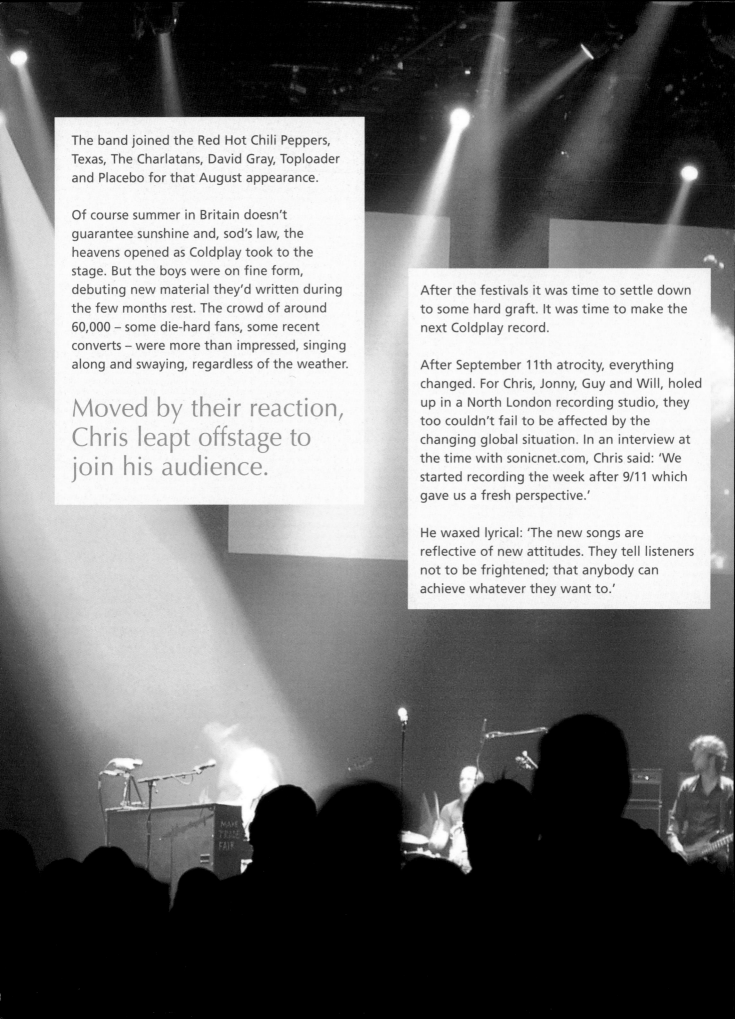

The band joined the Red Hot Chili Peppers, Texas, The Charlatans, David Gray, Toploader and Placebo for that August appearance.

Of course summer in Britain doesn't guarantee sunshine and, sod's law, the heavens opened as Coldplay took to the stage. But the boys were on fine form, debuting new material they'd written during the few months rest. The crowd of around 60,000 – some die-hard fans, some recent converts – were more than impressed, singing along and swaying, regardless of the weather.

Moved by their reaction, Chris leapt offstage to join his audience.

After the festivals it was time to settle down to some hard graft. It was time to make the next Coldplay record.

After September 11th atrocity, everything changed. For Chris, Jonny, Guy and Will, holed up in a North London recording studio, they too couldn't fail to be affected by the changing global situation. In an interview at the time with sonicnet.com, Chris said: 'We started recording the week after 9/11 which gave us a fresh perspective.'

He waxed lyrical: 'The new songs are reflective of new attitudes. They tell listeners not to be frightened; that anybody can achieve whatever they want to.'

Jonny and Chris had written over twenty songs for the new album, but eventually the track-listing would be whittled down to just eleven. After the recording sessions were over Chris sat back and listened to the entire album, which was titled: *A Rush of Blood to the Head*. All his fears and paranoia about whether he'd ever be able to write another song had been for nothing. The album was superb. Even Chris, the habitual doubting Thomas, knew that.

Glastonbury was *the* festival to play in the UK. Not so much for the profile it would offer a band, but for the whole experience. It was a reward after relentless touring and promotion; an event not just for the audience to enjoy, but for the bands as well.

Coldplay were lined up to headline the Pyramid Stage at Glastonbury 2002.

It was the year of the million pound security fence, after Glastonbury founder Michael Eavis had been reprimanded by his local council officials over the number of people that had jumped the fence in past years.

The critics were unequivocal in their praise: Coldplay had 'won' Glastonbury with their heady mix of *Parachutes* tracks and new material.

coldplay
glastonbury 2002

One famous face who was watching the show that day was the Australian singer and actress Natalie Imbruglia. Chris joked with a reporter afterwards saying he had fancied Natalie since she was in *Neighbours*, and that he'd blown his big chance.

You know when you really like someone and try to be funny. Well she ran away and thought I was stupid.

Two months later *A Rush of Blood to the Head* hit the record shop shelves. *The Mirror* said that with their second album and powerful live shows, Coldplay had finally won over any detractors.

Worldwide, the band had now sold five million copies of *Parachutes*, had been nominated - and won – countless awards including a Brit and a Grammy, but some people just couldn't understand why they didn't live the rock 'n' lifestyle. Which annoyed them. But since Coldplay had steadfastly refused to compromise, showing the world they were consistently able to write beautiful melodies, even their harshest critics gradually folded.

Chris had admitted he was more likely to be seen flying a kite than wrecking a hotel room. He told *Q Magazine* he had lost his virginity at 21. And drugs were as far removed from Coldplay's agenda as you could get. But it didn't matter. Not when you had just gone one better than the best album of 2000.

Chris met Gwyneth Paltrow at a party in New York in the autumn of 2002 and the rumour mill sprung into action almost straight away. Chris probably accepts that he had himself to blame for that one; when Gwyneth came to watch Coldplay at New York's Bowery Ballroom he dedicated the song 'In My Place' on the new album to her. As he sang the line 'I was scared, I was scared/ tired and under-prepared/ but I wait for you', any journalists at the gig must have been wetting themselves to get back to the office and bash out the copy for their celeb-hungry readers.

This time, the U.S tour to promote *A Rush of Blood* went smoothly. Chris didn't get sick and there were, thankfully, no rumours of a Coldplay split. Irish rockers Ash provided support for most of the dates and Coldplay flitted seamlessly between crowd pleasers 'Trouble' and 'Yellow', and songs from the new album.

Sipping ginger ale in a New York café, a by now exhausted Chris told a journalist America had been good to them: 'It's an amazing place. Just about everyone we've met here has been unbelievably cool.'

Everyone was... except Radiohead's Thom Yorke who blanked him in the lobby of a Los Angeles hotel. 'I was secretly a bit gutted,' Chris laughed.

I'm sure he knew I wasn't going to ask for his autograph. He recognised me.

Thorpe didn't know it but he'd tried pulling rank over someone who already out-ranked him.

The following month Gwyneth took friends to see the Coldplay gig at Wembley Arena. She was filming *Ted and Sylvia* – a film about the relationship between poets Sylvia Plath and Ted Hughes – in Cambridge at the time. Two weeks later she was spotted again, this time at the band's Dublin concert. But Coldplay's publicist continued to maintain the pair were 'just friends'. Earlier the same day Chris had popped into a late-night CD launch at Dublin's HMV store to buy five signed copies of the new David Gray album, *A New Day At Midnight*. Staff told him he could have them free of charge but he insisted in handing over some cash so they could buy themselves a drink. One of the CDs was a present for Gwyneth.

It was November before Chris admitted the pair were dating. When asked at the *Q Magazine* awards about the relationship he said:

'Gwyneth who?'

But the following weekend Chris would get his first taste of press intrusion. Heading out of his Hampstead apartment together on a Saturday night, they were snapped by a paparazzi photographer. The usually placid Chris was furious. 'Give me that film,' he shouted. 'Can't you just leave us alone?'

And while bookmakers Ladbrokes issued odds on the couple getting married in 2003, in some quarters doubt had set in. Some unkind 'friends' of Gwyneth told the press Chris was simply a 'stop-gap' to help the actress get over her father's death. Others claimed the match was made in heaven.

One tabloid reported that Gwyneth was 'zealous about healthy living and is said to be a homely girl who likes nothing more than a romantic night in.' If that was the case it was a perfect union.

Chris was hardly the sort of person likely to be spotted rolling blind drunk out of Soho House [aka Columbian House] at three in the morning.

But, as we know, Chris had begun to take his Fair Trade campaign very seriously. He signed up to be the face of the Oxfam's Make Trade Fair Campaign, kicking off with an appearance alongside British rapper Ms Dynamite for a duet at a charity concert at the London Astoria.

Make Trade Fair aims to give a voice to the farmers, labourers, and factory workers who are being cheated by what all the insiders know are the blatantly unfair rules of world trade.

One of the first things Chris agreed to do for the campaign was to have his photo taken whilst a sack of rice was being poured over his head. It was designed to draw attention to the fair trade issue and he joined actor Colin Firth (who was drenched in coffee), Alanis Morissette (buried in wheat), and Michael Stipe (who was covered in milk). It looked like Chris got away lightly.

The images were also designed to tell a story of how farmers in the third world were being 'dumped on' every day by rich countries. Chris was disgusted to learn how the US government pays its farmers $1billion a year to grow far more rice than they need and effectively 'dump' the surplus at super-cheap prices on poor countries. Thus the people living in those countries have no choice – they would rather buy the cheaper U.S-imported rice, while their farmers just can't compete.

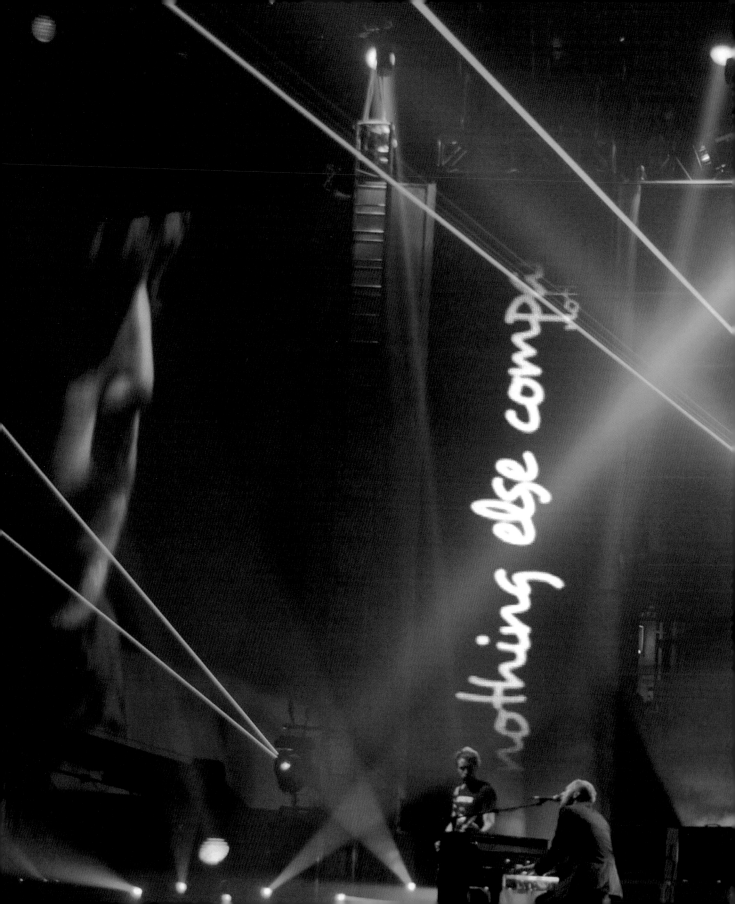

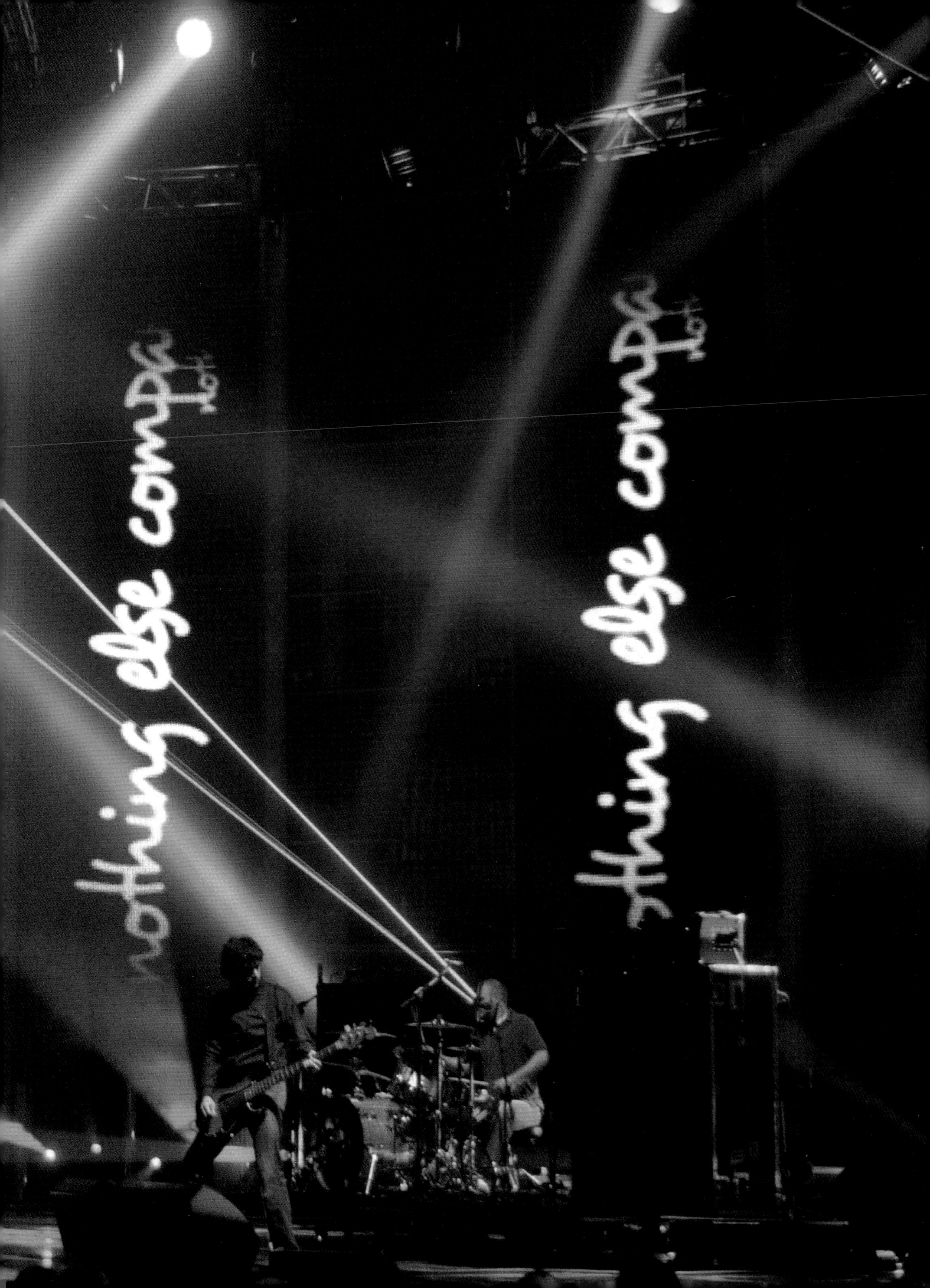

Chris and Gwyneth were finding it increasingly difficult to get on with their relationship under the persistent and blinding media spotlight. The *New York Post* (wrongly) claimed Gwyneth had dumped Chris as Coldplay started their North America tour.

When challenged at the *NME* awards, Chris told British reporters he was actually going out with Julia Roberts.

At the awards, Coldplay scooped the Best Album gong for *A Rush Of Blood*, which was also named Album of the Year by *NME* writers.

Punk rockers The Clash picked up the God Like Genius award. Dedicating the trophy to their charismatic lead singer Joe Strummer,

who had died a few months before, band member Paul Simonon took his place on the podium and said: 'This is for Joe. In the spirit of Joe and in the spirit of the Clash we say, "Don't Bomb Iraq".'

It was the beginning of a wave of bands and solo artists speaking out against the U.S and UK's decision to send bombs to Baghdad.

At the beginning of 2003 Chris took to the stage at London's Brit Awards ceremony where he accepted a trophy for *A Rush of Blood*: 'We are all going to die when George Bush has his way,' he told the audience, 'but at least we are going to go out with a bang.'

Chris left the stage that night to the roar of applause; he had never spoken publicly about Iraq before.

But his comments highlighted a growing number of British pop stars opposed to the military campaign. A petition published in *The Guardian*, carried the signatures of Craig David, Peter Gabriel, Brian Eno, Annie Lennox and Travis.

A week later Coldplay were in New York after being nominated for two Grammys, including best alternative music album for *A Rush of Blood*. A representative from the awards announced there would be no attempt to censor comments that Chris or any other trophy winner may want to make at the podium. But privately TV executives in the States were worried that the live broadcast in New York could turn into an anti-war rally. A senior CBS executive told one newspaper that microphones could be unplugged if the performance turned political.

While he was in New York Chris went on a walkabout through the streets with Gwyneth. Nothing strange about that, except the couple knew the media would be watching. And for the first time, they didn't care.

The band scooped two Grammys at the ceremony that weekend – the first group in history to win best alternative album two years running.

In March Chris announced his engagement to Gwyneth.

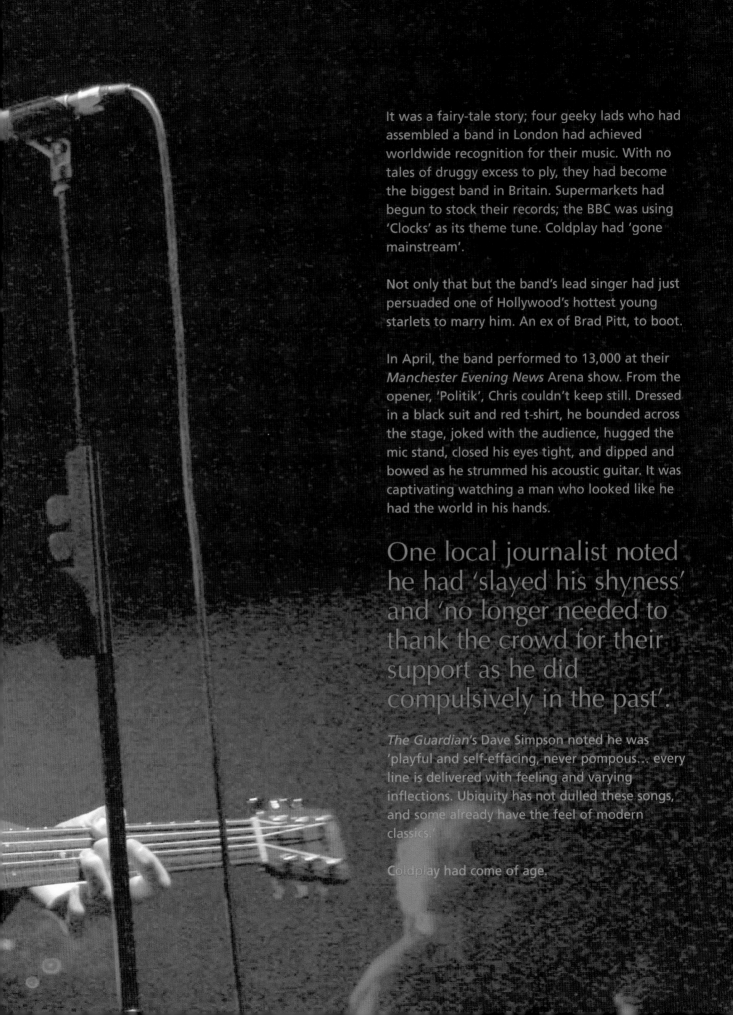

It was a fairy-tale story; four geeky lads who had assembled a band in London had achieved worldwide recognition for their music. With no tales of druggy excess to ply, they had become the biggest band in Britain. Supermarkets had begun to stock their records; the BBC was using 'Clocks' as its theme tune. Coldplay had 'gone mainstream'.

Not only that but the band's lead singer had just persuaded one of Hollywood's hottest young starlets to marry him. An ex of Brad Pitt, to boot.

In April, the band performed to 13,000 at their *Manchester Evening News* Arena show. From the opener, 'Politik', Chris couldn't keep still. Dressed in a black suit and red t-shirt, he bounded across the stage, joked with the audience, hugged the mic stand, closed his eyes tight, and dipped and bowed as he strummed his acoustic guitar. It was captivating watching a man who looked like he had the world in his hands.

One local journalist noted he had 'slayed his shyness' and 'no longer needed to thank the crowd for their support as he did compulsively in the past'.

The Guardian's Dave Simpson noted he was 'playful and self-effacing, never pompous... every line is delivered with feeling and varying inflections. Ubiquity has not dulled these songs, and some already have the feel of modern classics.'

Coldplay had come of age.

After playing a soaring version of 'Trouble', Chris boomed:

This is better than doing coke off a hooker's back! Which we don't do!

In their bizarre, inimitable way, and on their own terms, Coldplay had become rock 'n' roll stars – albeit in their conventionalism slightly eccentric rock 'n' roll stars.

A month later the band were chosen as song writers of the year at the Ivor Novello awards. Solo songwriter David Gray accepted the gong for best song of the year for his single 'The Other Side', while best contemporary song was won by Mike Skinner of The Streets for 'Weak Become Heroes'. Brian Wilson, the Beach Boys auteur was handed a special international award in the ceremony at the Grosvenor House Hotel.

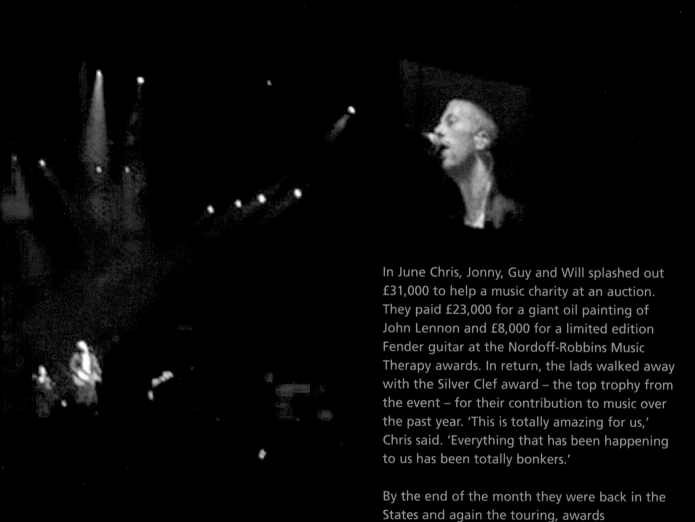

In June Chris, Jonny, Guy and Will splashed out
£31,000 to help a music charity at an auction.
They paid £23,000 for a giant oil painting of
John Lennon and £8,000 for a limited edition
Fender guitar at the Nordoff-Robbins Music
Therapy awards. In return, the lads walked away
with the Silver Clef award – the top trophy from
the event – for their contribution to music over
the past year. 'This is totally amazing for us,'
Chris said. 'Everything that has been happening
to us has been totally bonkers.'

By the end of the month they were back in the
States and again the touring, awards
ceremonies, interviews and appearances were
relentless.

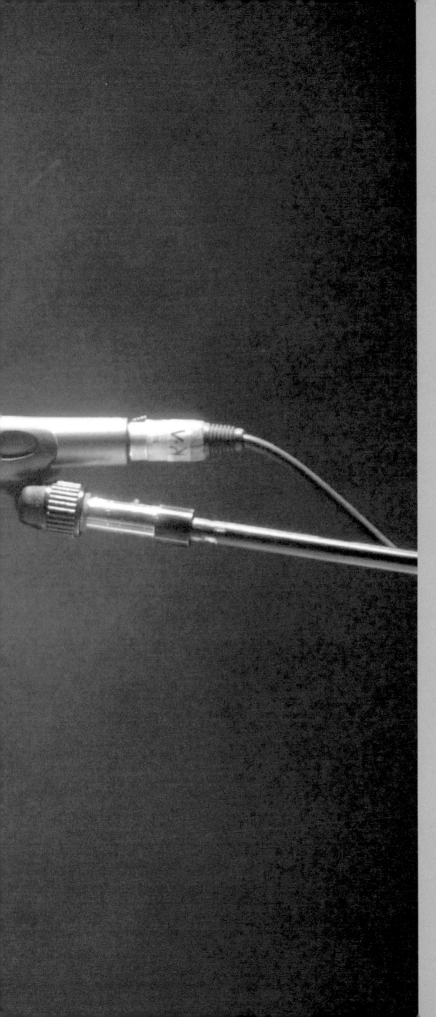

After a sold-out concert at the legendary Hollywood Bowl, the lads headed north to San Diego. 'I couldn't be happier,' Chris said. No longer feeling out of place sandwiched between heavy punk-pop acts on radio concert tours, Coldplay were finally doing it their way. Chris told the audience,

We want to fight to have sincere music be the main thing again.

As their San Diego gig pulled to a close, Guy, Will and Jonny left the stage, leaving Chris sitting in front of the piano, spotlight focused on his face as he launched into Louis Armstrong's classic 'What a Wonderful World'.

The *LA Times* said it was sung with a 'purity and faith that make you want to suspend disbelief and dream along. Whether backed by Jonny Buckland's jagged guitar licks or Martin's epic piano chords, the music is filled with such beauty and timeless grace that it reminds you of the purity of ancient cathedral bells.'

The words perfectly encapsulated Coldplay's music. Their songs were poetic and the new album, just like their debut, perfectly soundtracked their fans' lives.

Things were going remarkably well, but with Chris's new-found status as tabloid fodder, largely due to his relationship with Gwyneth, things were about to get nasty.

On a tour of Australia, a paparazzi photographer tried to get snaps of Chris surfing off Byron Bay, 500 miles north of Sydney on Australia's most easterly point. It's a popular tourist destination, with its glorious, unspoilt sandy beaches and azure sea populated by dolphins.

As the singer rushed up the sand in his wetsuit, he shouted at the photographer to give him the film. When the photographer refused, press reports claimed Chris smashed the windscreen of his car. He was later interviewed by police and a court hearing was set for October. But by November, Australian police had dropped the charges.

At least our bed-wetter-in-chief had shown that his wimpish image was for show. Chris is tougher than he acts.

In September the band took a day out of a short tour of South America to visit farmers in Mexico as part of Oxfam's Make Trade Fair campaign. Mexican farmers say they cannot compete with the huge subsidies afforded to their counterparts in the U.S.

On the trip, Chris and Jonny headed to the popular resort town of Cancun to present the World Trade Organisation with a three million signature strong petition demanding an end to agricultural dumping and export subsidies. Chris was emphatic about their role:

We see ourselves as a billboard for an idea, not as the solution.

To emphasise his commitment to the Make Trade Fair campaign, Chris scrawls an 'equals' sign onto his left hand in black felt-tip pen to symbolise equality in trade. While the rest of the band obviously share his compassion, it is Chris who brings the subject up at every opportunity and there are no inky marks on any of the limbs belonging to Jonny, Will or Guy.

On a fact-finding mission to Ghana with Oxfam, the aeroplane Chris was travelling on got into difficulties. Afterwards he told reporters, 'I thought "I'll be dying on a Fair Trade trip so at least people will always link me with that".' He feels as passionately about Fair Trade as Bob Geldof does debt relief.

And if drummer Will thought he could escape the media by sitting at the back of the stage, he was sorely mistaken.

The *Sunday Mirror* broke the story that he had become embroiled in a row with his next door neighbour in Kennington, South London. Will lived in the Georgian house with his fiancée Mariana.

One evening he had booked a taxi – through his record company – but unbeknown to him, so had

his neighbour, Jacqueline. When the cab arrived, Jacqueline took it but it was only when the cab driver realised his destination had changed that she discovered what had happened.

She left a note for Will apologising but was shocked to receive a letter from the band's solicitors, accusing her of `deception' and `theft'.

Will was becoming a bit prima donna-ish in his stardom. This particular PR disaster was quicky resolved but it showed the band how easily they could give the press an excuse to turn on them.

Despite the unwanted media attention, Chris's relationship with Gwyneth didn't hurt the band's profile. *A Rush of Blood* sold more than two million copies and the north American tour grossed £4.3 million.

U2's Bono claimed Chris was his successor in the global fight for fairer trade. Liam Gallagher, on the other hand, wasn't impressed. 'What's all that with writing messages about Free Trade on his hand,' he said. 'If he wants to write things down I'll give him a fucking pen and paper. Bunch of fucking students'

At the beginning of December Chris and Gwyneth announced they were having a baby, due in summer 2004. Four days later they married in secret at a register office in Santa Barbara, California in a short ceremony. Their honeymoon was in Mexico, at an exclusive beach complex.

2004 started with a bang. Once again, Coldplay were at the Grammys, this time walking away with the coveted Record of the Year award for 'Clocks', dashing the hopes of a six-years-in-a-row gong for Beyonce Knowles. The year before Chris had held his tongue on the contentious issue of the war. This year he didn't care.

'We would like to dedicate this to Johnny Cash and to John Kerry, who hopefully will be your president some day,' he told the star-studded crowd.

Afterwards CNN claimed Kerry 'couldn't have drawn better publicity if he had staged a wardrobe malfunction with Justin Timberlake.'

Not that the endorsement did Kerry much good.

Of course his comments were controversial – particularly in an America as divided as it was over the Iraq war and the presidential nominees.

Organisers of the Grammys were desperate to avoid controversy after Janet Jackson had bared her breast at the end of a live duet with Justin Timberlake at the Super Bowl only one week before.

Nudity and politics are frowned upon by the event's broadcasters as the show is screened early enough for kids to watch. Plus international bands are ill-advised to comment on U.S politics if they're trying to break America. Still, Chris's comments didn't seem to do Coldplay any harm. And you got the impression that they really couldn't care less if they did.

Will later said: 'I think getting involved in party politics can be a dangerous area. That's people's freedom to choose. The things we stand for are world issues that are completely apart from party politics.'

Other award winners that night were OutKast, who took home Grammys for best album and best rap

album for *Speakerboxxx/The Love Below*, plus a gong for best urban/alternative performance for 'Hey Ya!' Christian rockers Evanescence won best new artist, and Beyonce claimed five Grammys including best contemporary rhythm and blues album.

The Beatles won a special President's Award for their contribution to popular music. Ringo Starr accepted it and in his speech pointed out,

No-one can imagine these days what an incredible feat it was to conquer America. No British act had done it before.

Of course his words resonated slightly more that he perhaps expected. Coldplay were in the process of doing exactly the same thing. And it was still no mean feat, even though it nearly forty years on from when the Beatles blazed the trail.

The Independent newspaper ran a story shortly afterwards aiming to get to the bottom of how 'Coldplay became the coolest band in America'. In Britain, the journalist wrote,

Martin is seen as a 'neo-nerd' pop star who likes wearing woolly hats. But in America, Coldplay are seen as cutting edge alternative rock.

Mojo's editor, Phil Alexander, offered his theory: 'Coldplay offer something different to the great American record-buying public,' he said. 'They're seen as an extension of Radiohead as part of an alternative rock lineage.'

The *NME*'s Alex Needham, said in Britain there was always a suspicion of people who went off with Hollywood stars.

The British attitude to its brightest and best has always been the same. We have a habit of knocking our stars down when they get too big. Perhaps what Coldplay needed was another album – one even better than the last – to convince their detractors once and for all.

By April Chris and Gwyneth had hit the headlines again when papers reported he had lashed out at a photographer trying to get photos of his pregnant wife as they left London's San Lorenzo restaurant. Chris denied attacking him and Coldplay's spokesman said the photographer tripped while chasing Gwyneth's taxi in Knightsbridge. He eventually accepted a police caution but the event only served to prove how very un-wimpy Chris was becoming in the face of press intrusion.

On May 14th, Gwyneth gave birth to Apple Blythe Alison Martin. She was born in London, weighing nine pounds, eleven ounces.

Soon after, dressed like Spinal Tap and with Chris sporting a rather scary blonde mullet wig, the band recorded an impromptu performance under the pseudonym 'The Nappies' – a paean to Gwyneth giving birth to Apple.

They put in on Coldplay website, which announced: 'In celebration of the birth of Apple Blythe Alison Martin, we are pleased to introduce you to another new arrival. Please click on of the links below to see the latest addition to the Coldplay camp'. A simple click revealed the hilarious result of a few hours mis-spent in the studio.
'I ain't no baddie/ I ain't no baddie/ I am your baby's daddy,' bellows a rather disturbed-looking Chris into the mike. 'Your cup's gone up from an A to D/ that's bad for you but it's fun for me… I'll be there with you baby/ through the thin and the thick/ I'm gonna clean up all the poo and the sick.'

It was all a bit of probably drunken fun. Twelve days later Chris, Jonny, Guy and Will were photographed taking her for a walk through a London park, taking charge while Gwyneth had a well-deserved rest.

As for her movie career, Gwyneth, said she was going to put it on hold, despite being one of Hollywood's best-loved stars, so she could devote herself to her new baby and husband.

She had wrapped up filming *Proof*, directed by John Madden – a film about a daughter who comes to the aid of her dying maths professor father – now she decided to take time out to enjoy motherhood.

Devoting time to their personal lives again gave the band a chance to rest and write songs for the new album. This time the recording process was very different. Chris and Jonny had flown to Chicago to work on some demos. When they returned to the UK they planned to use the recordings as templates. Each member of Coldplay would go into the studio alone and lay their individual parts down. Will would go in, lay his drum tracks down, and go home. Then it was Guy's turn, followed by Jonny, and lastly Chris. But it was a very disjointed way of working and after the album was completed it sounded wrong.

Something was missing. Sure, there were some big songs – numbers they were rightly proud of – but some just sounded flat and too processed; like they were just going through the motions.

'It didn't sound like a band that was playing together in a room, which is what great records should sound like,' Will said.

And that was exactly the reason it sounded the way it did. They hadn't played together in a room for an awfully long time. 'We realised we needed to hire a little rehearsal room and play these songs together until we knew how they sounded best,' Will said. 'We had to be reminded we didn't need this big flashy studio and lots of assistants running around. We didn't have that when we first started to play music together and that was something we needed to recapture.'

The band weren't coy about admitting this was what was holding them back either. Chris told one journalist that he thought finishing off the new album was making him go bald.

When my hair's gone back another inch, I know we'll have finished our album.

He added, 'We're under an immense amount of intense pressure in the studio.' Presumably Chris' follicles were, too.

After the revelation that they just needed to spend some time playing the songs live in a small studio as a band, Chris, Jonny, Guy and Will became inseparable again.

The band's work to promote fair trade and draw attention to the situation in Africa was also gathering pace. Then, as 2004 drew to a close, it was announced Coldplay would be joining The Darkness and Travis to re-record Band Aid's hit single 'Do They Know It's Christmas'.

And overnight it became the odds-on favourite for the coveted Christmas No 1 slot.

Midge Ure, one of the original organisers of Band Aid, and a driving force behind the latest effort, observed...

Chris Martin reminds me of a young Bono.

'What's frightening though is most of (these bands) were in nappies first time around!'

Now, they were changing them...
...well Chris was.

MAKE TRADE FAIR

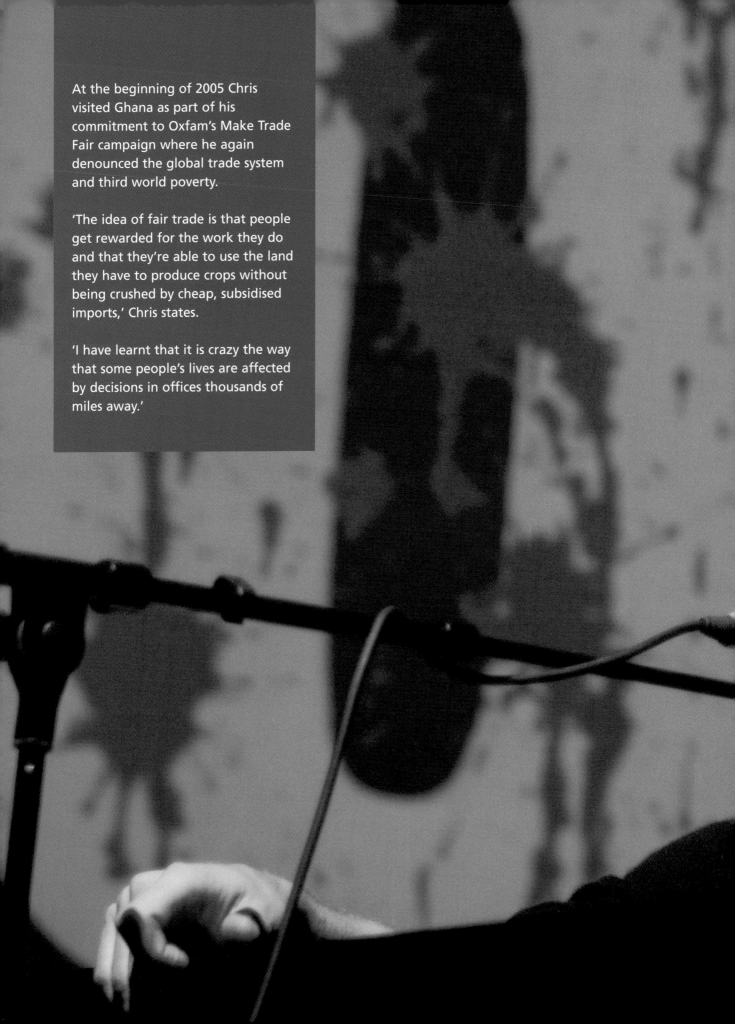

At the beginning of 2005 Chris visited Ghana as part of his commitment to Oxfam's Make Trade Fair campaign where he again denounced the global trade system and third world poverty.

'The idea of fair trade is that people get rewarded for the work they do and that they're able to use the land they have to produce crops without being crushed by cheap, subsidised imports,' Chris states.

'I have learnt that it is crazy the way that some people's lives are affected by decisions in offices thousands of miles away.'

Africa suffers from that terribly – whether it's cotton in Mozambique or rice in Ghana. And we have to keep talking about it. We regard it as the same as Beyoncé's commitment to Loreal.

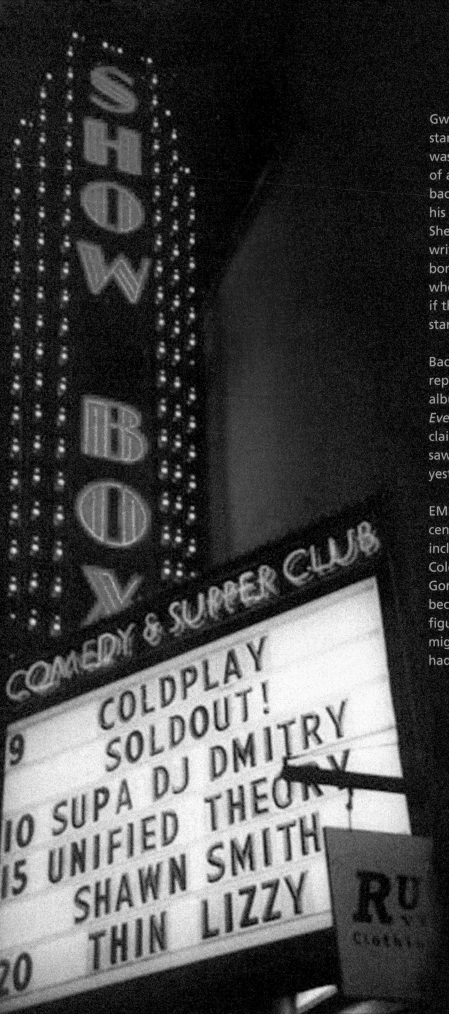

Gwyneth soon resumed her acting career, starting with *Running With Scissors*, which was based on the darkly comedic memoirs of author Augusten Burroughs, who looks back on his unconventional childhood with his unbalanced mother and alcoholic father. She also signed up for a project about writer Truman Capote based on the close bond he'd established with two murderers when he was researching, *In Cold Blood*. As if that wasn't enough, she also accepted the starring role in a biopic of Marlene Dietrich.

Back in the UK, the press were universally reporting the delay of Coldplay's new album. 'It has sent EMI into a spin,' the *Evening Standard* reported. *The Express* claimed, 'Britain's largest record company saw 16 per cent wiped off its value yesterday.'.

EMI's share price had dropped by 16 per cent but it was for a variety of reasons – including delayed albums from both Coldplay and Damon Albarn's alter ego Gorrilaz. The albums would be released, but because it was the end of the fiscal year, the figures just didn't look as healthy as they might have done for 2004/5 if the albums had been released on time.

Will, for one, didn't seem to care. 'Record companies in general are not doing very well at the moment and their share prices are going to fall,' he pointed out. 'EMI wanted to equate their share price fall to our album being late because it was a temporary thing. It was like saying "you do know it is going to come out in a few weeks time so hopefully share prices are going to go up".

'We don't feel any pressure to make them money. If they don't feel we're doing a good enough job then they'll drop us and we'll have no record contract, which will be f***ing brilliant. You always hear about people who have these huge court battles to get out of their record contract and it would mean we're completely free to do whatever we wanted to do – no contractual obligations or whatever.

We'd just be free to release our own records on the internet. And so we don't worry about the album being late to be honest.

Guy, though, was quick to stress the band still had a great relationship with their record label: 'These figures come from money-man accountants sitting at the top of an office, somewhere that we have no contact with. And anyway that stuff is peripheral – a distraction and nothing more than that. Our album wasn't ready, so we weren't going to give it to them. And to be fair Parlophone told us to take as long as we needed. They said that they didn't want a half-baked record just to fit into their fiscal calendar.'

The new album – *X&Y* – was finally delivered to Parlophone in early April and mooted for a June release.

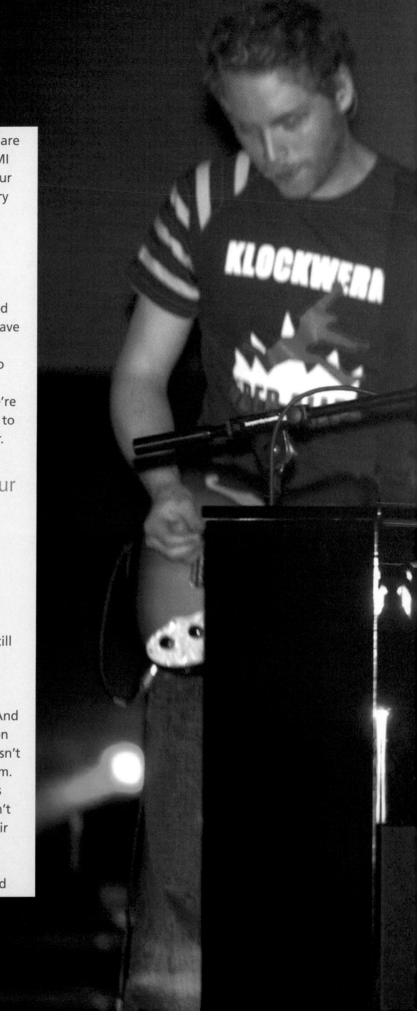

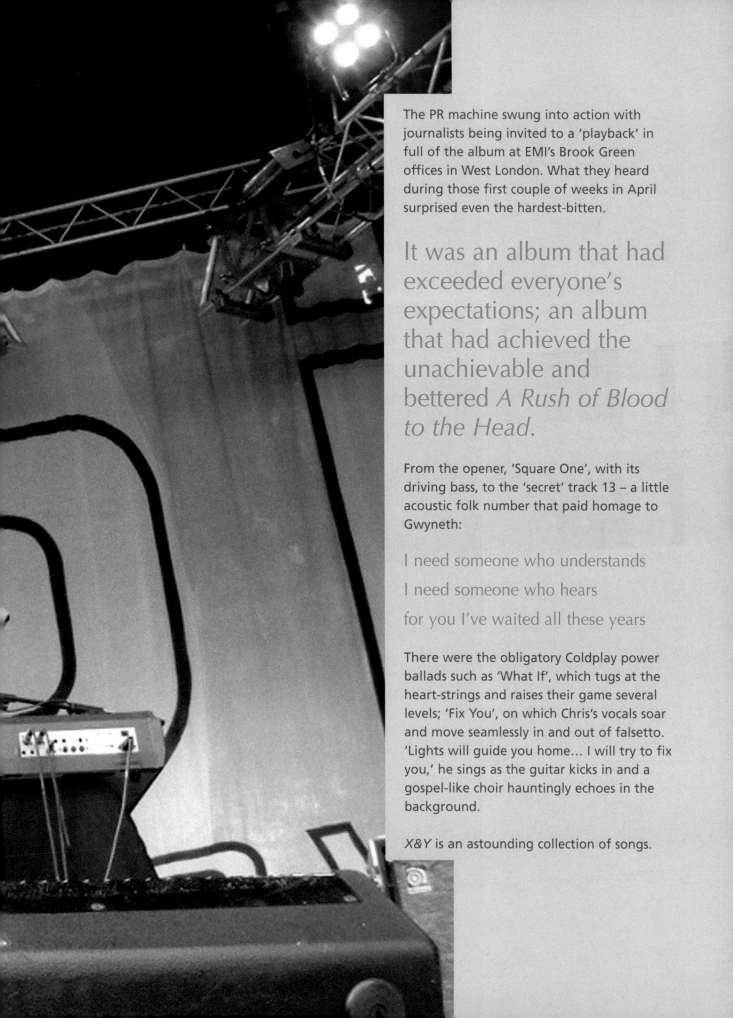

The PR machine swung into action with journalists being invited to a 'playback' in full of the album at EMI's Brook Green offices in West London. What they heard during those first couple of weeks in April surprised even the hardest-bitten.

It was an album that had exceeded everyone's expectations; an album that had achieved the unachievable and bettered *A Rush of Blood to the Head*.

From the opener, 'Square One', with its driving bass, to the 'secret' track 13 – a little acoustic folk number that paid homage to Gwyneth:

I need someone who understands

I need someone who hears

for you I've waited all these years

There were the obligatory Coldplay power ballads such as 'What If', which tugs at the heart-strings and raises their game several levels; 'Fix You', on which Chris's vocals soar and move seamlessly in and out of falsetto. 'Lights will guide you home… I will try to fix you,' he sings as the guitar kicks in and a gospel-like choir hauntingly echoes in the background.

X&Y is an astounding collection of songs.

It has impeccable production qualities and each song could be a single. On 'Swallowed in the Sea', Chris's vocals are so close it's like he's in the room with you.

The song, 'A Message', apparently came to Chris as a revelation in the middle of the night. According to him...

It's our Archimedes song.

He explained, 'But whereas Archimedes jumped out the bath and said "Eureka", I jumped out of bed and said "I've got to go downstairs and write this down." Mine wasn't quite as glamorous.

'All songs come from somewhere I don't understand – some crazy place. There's so much we don't understand in this world, so to write it off as meaningless would be incredibly foolish. So in that sense I definitely believe in something.'

Despite Coldplay's incredible success, they could still count on living regular lives outside of the glamour of the music industry for inspiration. 'We just had to be careful to edit certain things out,' Chris laughed. 'Some things you feel as a pop star are exactly the same as you would feel if you were a dustman or a cleaner. And Jon and I should know because we both used to be cleaners. Similarly it's harder for people to relate to you if you're singing about sitting behind Beyoncé at the MTV awards – which is also in our experience.

We've got to appreciate we're just jammy to be here in the first place.

X&Y gives an unmistakeable nod to 1980s bands like New Order, The Cure and Kraftwerk. It is also louder, rockier in places than *Parachutes* or *A Rush of Blood*, yet the melodies are always there – either obvious in the simplicity of a piano or acoustic guitar, or subtly buried in a wall of overdrive ensemble.

'Sonically it's an attempt to plagiarise from as many places as possible and New Order and Kraftwerk were some of the first places we stopped,' Chris said, laughing.

Jonny added,

In terms of the heaviness we just wanted to **turn the contrast up** on this one, make it more dynamic than previous albums.

On *X&Y*, Coldplay's voice is louder than ever. The band have been determined to stamp their indelible mark onto the songs. On an upbeat song they're happier than they've ever been. On a downbeat song, they're sadder than ever. On *X&Y* they express themselves clearer than ever before. According to Chris...

There's no point being timid.

In one sense they're more confident but, as always with the band, what drives them on is the constant worry about whether what they've done is actually good enough. There's a persistent desire to better themselves and it seems that'll never change.